MW01126956

Zelda's Odyssey

Cathy Albright Ryker

Zelda's Odyssey is a heartwarming chronicle of an orphan cat's love of adventure and search for happiness in an insecure world, where cats think and act like people, and people interact with cats like – well, like people.

Zelda's Odyssey

by

Cathy Albright Kyker

Cover and Illustrations

by

Linda Wunder

Copyright © 2023 by Cathy Albright Kyker

All rights reserved. No part of this book may be used or reproduced in any manner whatsoever without written permission from Cathy Albright Kyker, St. Simons Island, GA.

ISBN-13: 979-8-218-18246-5

Printed in the United States of America

For

STAN and CHERIE

Prologue

Zelda could see something was troubling her mother. Zora had been quiet and pensive for several days, very different from her normal happy-go-lucky and outgoing personality. What Zelda did not know was that Zora was trying to decide if it was time to leave Zelda and her brothers, Zeke and Zach, to live on their own.

This struggle was giving Zora a major heartache. Should she travel and see the world, as she had always wanted? How would her brood handle the separation? She was especially concerned about Zelda, the smallest and most vulnerable of the three. They were doing well as a family; she wondered what would happen if she left? On the other hand, she had watched them all mature in such positive ways that she could not imagine a situation they wouldn't be able to handle.

After vacillating back and forth, Zora came to a conclusion. She knew what to do. She told her children how much she loved them and said it was time for them to make their own way in the world. She planned to leave them where they were born, in the lovely trailer park of Pine Needle, known for its grandiose oak trees and a few scattered pines. Zora knew it was a safe and secure place for cats because most residents were cat lovers.

Zelda was surprised and shocked when she heard Zora's plans. She had an overwhelming sense of sadness and fear. "What? Mom's leaving? What will I do now? Will Zach and Zeke leave me too?" Zora reassured all three that they were strong, capable, and above all, they had each other. She was confident they were ready. Besides, having been raised in

Pine Needle herself, Zora could think of no better place to leave her family.

Zora would never see her children again. She would never know that one son would be honored with Hollywood's exclusive *Cat Model of the Year* award nor would she know that the other would become a famous mice hockey coach. Zora would also be spared the knowledge of Zelda's many harrowing and life-threatening adventures.

Chapter 1

Zelda was a small eight-pound black and white tuxedo cat. Her black nose and the uneven white markings on either side of it seemed to form a mischievous smile on her muzzle. Zelda also had a small patch of white fur on her back that fooled many a painter into believing he'd dropped that dab of white on her.

Her brothers, Zeke and Zach, had grown to be larger cats, each weighing a hefty 15 pounds. Zeke was a gorgeous black and white cat with perfect tuxedo markings. He adored Zelda and was especially protective of her because of her small size. Zach was the jokester of the family, making them laugh even when he played pranks on his siblings. The brothers were the best of friends.

Still, Zeke was a wee bit envious of Zach. An orange tabby with a white vest, Zach was a polydactyl known for his huge white front paws that had six toes each! Everyone (people and cats alike) admired him, especially Zeke. "What I wouldn't do to have those paws," thought Zeke. Zach was, as they say, "The Man."

After Zora left to explore the world, Mark, a retired restaurant chef, moved to Pine Needle. He moved there because of the relaxed environment and massive oak trees, but he soon became enamored with what he called the "3 Z's." They responded with charm and affection.

In relationships between cats and people, charm is a two-way street. Cats do their part by entertaining people with their antics, being playful, allowing people to pet and hold them (which most cats like anyway) and returning affection. The siblings were masters of charm and totally beguiled Mark.

People do their part by rewarding cats for their behavior: feeding and petting them, letting them sit on their laps, providing cat toys, talking nicely and often letting them live inside their homes. That was the case with Mark except for one thing: He did not allow the "3 Z's" to come into his trailer because he didn't like to vacuum cat hair. So, while becoming an integral part of Mark's life, they remained "outdoor cats."

The siblings were like the three musketeers, "All for one and one for all." When Zelda was a year old, a larger cat named

Missy tried to take her food. Zeke and Zach stepped in and told Missy to find another plate. Afterwards, they told Zelda she had to learn to defend herself and began instructing her in the art of standing her ground. They suggested she take an attitude to intimidate an opponent before anything physical happened. "Flatten your ears, lash your tail back and forth, hunch up your back, hiss and act like you will attack."

The brothers also taught Zelda psychological skills she could use to protect herself, such as pretending to give up. "When the other cat lets down its guard, use that moment for a surprise attack," Zach said.

A third component of the boys' training was to teach Zelda basic martial arts techniques, pointing out vulnerable areas all cats have, such as the neck and stomach. "Lying on your back will give you access to your opponent's underbelly. Use your back paws to 'bunny kick' your opponent in the stomach." Zelda listened, practiced, and learned.

Afterwards, when other cats tried to take her food, Zelda used this new approach. She surprised even herself at how successful the new tactics were. Rarely did she have to do more than threaten the aggressors. But if those cats didn't leave soon enough and needed another reminder to "BE GONE," Zelda simply gave them a light punch with her paw, and they let the matter settle in her favor.

Chapter 2

Months later, a huge cat named Growler wandered into Pine Needle. Weighing five pounds more than the largest cats in the neighborhood, Growler enjoyed strutting through the trailer park, showing off his muscular power and doing what he did best: being evil and menacing. He was often seen pouncing on more vulnerable cats just to show off his size and strength.

Growler became infamous as the "Pine Needle Bully." He pushed cats from their food and ate it himself, all the while laughing as his victims cringed in fear. Growler was also known to chase cats away from their own living areas just for the fun of it. Some cats resisted but quickly backed down when Growler exhibited his violent and aggressive behavior.

Zelda's **first major life adventure** began with a confrontation with Growler. Some cats just don't like to work for a living and can be quite nasty when trying to get what they want. Growler was one of them. Devoid of the charm that Zelda, her brothers, and many other cats possessed, he had no skill in enticing people to offer him decent food, much less offer him a home. Growler waited for other cats to earn their food with their charm and then he would steal it from them.

One day, Growler awoke from a long catnap and was on the move to find his dinner when he spotted Zelda. She had just earned a plate of leftover chicken and green beans from Mark before he left to run errands. Zelda was alone when she sat down to eat. Her brothers were several trailers away playing mice hockey: using their paws to hit a toy mouse down a narrow lane toward an empty and upended box.

Zelda looked up and saw Growler moving toward her, his eyes fixed on her food. He flexed his gigantic muscles and glared at her. Although Zelda had been quite confident in her defensive tactics and martial arts skills, that confidence was shaken when she saw up close just how big Growler was. Still, Zelda didn't want to give up Mark's delicious cuisine. She had been taught to stand her ground and this looked like the perfect test to see if she could actually do it.

Swaggering, Growler continued toward Zelda and her food. He believed that since she was young and small, it would be a snap to steal her meal. Growler expected Zelda to run away. Instead, she hunched her back and hissed at him. Perturbed, Growler made horrible long growling and hissing sounds. Then he made even louder screeching noises, which were particularly scary for most creatures.

Zelda was shocked and a bit frightened by Growler's actions but she remained calm. She whimpered, took a few steps away from him and pretended to give up, as her brothers had taught her. She provided Growler with a clear path to her dinner. Growler thought, "Good, she's backed away." He walked right past Zelda, leaving his side and rear vulnerable.

The moment Growler got within a foot of Zelda's food, she vaulted into the air and landed on his back. Growler swung around to throw her off, but she clawed into him and rode him like a cowboy riding a bronco. Growler couldn't shake her. Zelda bit him on the neck and he yowled in pain. Trying to ignore the torment and get the food he came for, Growler turned toward the plate with Zelda still on his back. She jumped to the ground and found Growler's underbelly. Zelda "bunny kicked" her back paws into him so hard he could barely breathe.

Gasping, Growler thought, "Oh man, I'm not going to work this hard to steal a punk cat's food, especially a punk girl cat." Zelda continued pumping her feet, clawing, and biting him until he finally broke and ran. Zelda won!!

Humiliated by his defeat, Growler never returned to Pine Needle. The many cats who had watched the fight were in-credulous at the outcome. Zelda had earned the reputation of being "the cat who battled and beat Growler, the Pine Needle Bully" and she was hailed as a heroine in the trailer park.

Zach and Zeke were amazed and proud that Zelda had fended off such a big bully. They were now assured she had the necessary survival skills to care for herself and they no longer worried about her size and weight.

Mark heard about Zelda's victory from neighbors and was surprised and pleased. He praised her and checked her for injuries. Mark found her paws were sore and tender and realized one of her claws had been lost in the fracas. A cat's claws grow back quickly, so there was no need for worry. Zelda's first adventure was a success.

HOLLYWOOD

Chapter 3

A year later, Mark was visited by his friends, the Zieglers, who lived in Hollywood, California. They were cat lovers and had recently lost the last of their many cats. The Zieglers always took their cats with them when they traveled in their RV, so this journey without even one of their beloved fur babies was lonely and difficult.

The Zieglers' cats had always been their main priority in life. They gave them excellent food, first-rate cat toys, exciting travel experiences and only the best professional veterinarian services. From Mabel to Blackie, to Franny and Tobie and more, all were special and dearly loved. The "kids," as they called them, came first no matter what it cost, and the Zieglers worked hard to provide for them.

Upon meeting Zach, Zeke, and Zelda, the Zieglers were drawn to all of them. But the more they came to know Zeke, the more smitten they became with this loving, kind, and handsome cat. While at Pine Needle, they doted on him and let him stay in their RV. Six weeks later, Zeke returned to Hollywood with them.

It was a sorrowful parting for Zeke's siblings as they said their goodbyes, but they were happy for their brother. They knew the Zieglers were committed to caring for him. Zach and Zelda still had Mark to watch over them. Even though they were left out of Mark's trailer night and day, they were well-fed and had great times with their benefactor.

Zeke's arrival in Hollywood changed the Zieglers lives forever. They knew famous actors, musicians, and other luminaries in "the biz." An agent who specialized in celebrity cats encouraged them to let Zeke try out as a model.

He was an instant success. Zeke's picture started showing up on billboards and in magazines and bestselling calendars, and he even appeared in several movies. He became a regular on the red carpet with human models and actors and easily won Hollywood's prestigious *"Cat Model of the Year"* award.

So many offers were coming in that the Zieglers had to quit their regular jobs to manage Zeke's career. They had taken this stray cat in simply because they loved him and wanted to care for him. They never imagined that he would wind up taking care of them and making them wealthy beyond their wildest dreams.

Chapter 4

Back in Pine Needle, things weren't nearly as rosy. An unhappy, bitter young man named Brutus visited the trailer park thinking he might want to move there. He hated cats and would have killed them all if he could. But Brutus could see how well-regarded the Pine Needle cats were and knew better than to hurt any of them. Instead, before he left, he anonymously called Animal Control and claimed the place was overrun with cats that were overbreeding, unlicensed, and had rabies, fleas and ear mites. Most of his allegations were false, but it was true that many of the cats, like Zelda, were unlicensed.

When Animal Control responded to Brutus's complaint, Zelda's **second adventure** began. She was lying under an oak tree not far from Mark's trailer and before she could flee, Zelda was scooped up along with six other unlicensed cats. Mark wasn't there to intervene because he had flown to Hollywood to visit Zeke and the Zieglers.

When the Pine Needle captives arrived at the jail-pound, Zelda was thrown into a cat kennel with 45 strangers, male and female. She didn't even know the six cats from Pine Needle who were apprehended with her because her brothers had always cautioned her to be wary of other cats.

But the captured Pine Needle cats certainly knew of Zelda. She had been held in high esteem by many in Pine Needle ever since the Growler incident. However, two of the new cat convicts were wickedly jealous, not only of Zelda's status but also of the gourmet meals that Mark fed her. They openly mocked her with remarks such as "Now 'Miss Perfect Punch' gets to eat plain dry cat food like everybody else."

Nevertheless, one of the Pine Needle cats had long admired Zelda. Her name was Frida.

Chapter 5

Frida was black and white like Zelda, but instead of tuxedo markings, her black legs had vertical white stripes. She also sported a Groucho Marx mustache. Frida weighed only six pounds, much smaller than Zelda.

Like Zelda, Frida had lived her entire life in Pine Needle. Until the last few months before she was incarcerated in the jail-pound, Frida resided with a caring people family. Sadly, they were evicted from their trailer and in the chaos, Frida was left behind. Other Pine Needle cats told Frida how her mommy, daddy and their children had frantically searched everywhere for her and left the trailer park in tears when they couldn't find her. That information was of little comfort to Frida because there was no getting around the fact that the life she had lived and loved was over.

Frida now found herself sad, alone, scared and with limited survival skills. What she didn't realize was that the love and security she had enjoyed with her human family had built a strong internal foundation in her that would see her through this and every other challenge she would face.

Frida was remarkably kind and nice to other cats, so in no time, she made several cat friends. She avoided altercations with larger meaner cats. Her people skills were outstanding. Soon she was charming many residents of Pine Needle and having fun and entertaining times with them. Most rewarded her with meals and treats, but unfortunately, none offered her a spot in their family.

Prior to becoming acquainted with each other in the jail-pound, Frida and Zelda were strangers. Frida had witnessed the fight between Zelda and Growler; and after Zelda won, Frida had admired Zelda from afar. Frida was amazed that Zelda could win such a David & Goliath type fight. She wondered if she would have had the courage to even face up to a cruel, strong bully, much less win the battle. Now Zelda and Frida found themselves in the same predicament: both were prisoners in the jail-pound.

Chapter 6

The contrast between Frida and Zelda could not have been more striking. Zelda was wary of other cats, kept her distance, was considered standoffish and had lived her entire life as an outdoors cat. Conversely, Frida had numerous cat friends, had been raised as a beloved cat in a human family home and it felt natural for her to be trusting of people and other cats.

The more Zelda and Frida got to know each other, the more this unlikely relationship blossomed into a close friendship. The two of them would hang out, eat their meals together, share jokes and laugh. But they also commiserated about their predicament and wondered if they would ever return to their beloved Pine Needle, or at least get out of the jail-pound.

Frida desperately wanted a family. She told Zelda all about sitting on her Mommy's lap and being held by family members. She said her Daddy fed her twice a day. Frida also shared that she slept in a bed with one of the children and was hugged and petted to sleep every night. She played and roamed in Pine Needle during the day before coming home at dusk to enjoy her family time. She recalled that each night before going to bed, her Mommy threw cat treats down the hallway and Frida chased and ate each one, laughing at this great game. She deeply missed her "perfect family." Who wouldn't?

People came to the jail-pound every day to look at the cats through a glass-barred window; but all the larger cats hogged the limited space at the window. Since Frida and Zelda could not find a place to be seen, their beauty and charming personalities were virtually invisible.

Frequently one of the larger cats would be taken out for a people visit. Often, those same people would come back the next day and take the cat home. But Zelda and Frida never had a chance. Zelda thought for sure that her Pine Needle benefactor, Mark, would come liberate her. As the days wore on and he failed to appear, Zelda became despondent. Frida pined for a new family and was extremely depressed about her situation. The rejection was getting to both of them, but at least they had each other.

Ten days into this nightmare, the 12-pound cats were taking catnaps when new people came to look through the window.

Zelda seized the opportunity. She leapt to the window, pushed a 10-pound male off the sill, and told Frida to hurry and join her. Finally, they were going to be seen!

Frida was immediately noticed and taken out for her first people visit. When she returned, she couldn't wait to tell the other cats all about it. Her visitors were a family with children and all of them seemed to like her. Could this be the start of her return to a perfect life? Wouldn't it be terrific if they lived in Pine Needle?

Chapter 7

Zelda loved hearing about Frida's visitors and seeing how excited she was. But the realization of what this could mean hit them both at the same time. If the family did return and offer Frida a home, these best friends would be separated, maybe forever. There was no more talk about the people visit. They were panic stricken.

Zelda and Frida needed to be alone, which, of course, was impossible in their situation. The only accommodation they could find was an unoccupied corner of their cell. There they had a heart-to-heart talk.

Frida told Zelda how much she admired her and how great a role model she was for her. She would never forget Zelda's advice on how to stand up for herself and face challenges. Frida said life in the jail-pound would have been unbearable without her devoted friend.

Zelda returned the affection. She said Frida had taught her how to have a friend and be a friend. She realized she didn't have to be alone. Zelda had learned from Frida how to develop relationships and bond with cats as well as people. The shell Zelda had built around herself was not nearly as hard as it had been. They both laughed and cried when Zelda said, "Frida, you're such a schweeta!"

They hugged for a long time before either of them could say another word. They vowed to be friends forever, even if they never saw each other again. No matter what happened in the future, they would both know how the other felt about their relationship. It had been obvious from the first day that the jail-pound was not where they nor any other cats belonged. They had to get out of this place if it was the last thing they ever did. Getting out of the jail-pound became paramount.

For two days, more people visited the jail-pound but as usual, the larger cats blocked the entire window. Neither Zelda nor Frida were able to be seen. The next morning, when Zelda awakened, Frida was gone. One of the other Pine Needle cats meowed loudly, "She got her family." Zelda was in shock. After she and Frida had their special talk and said their good-byes, Zelda thought she could take living in the jail-pound without Frida. But that was then. Now that it had actually happened, Zelda was paralyzed by her grief.

After sobbing over the loss of Frida, Zelda began to reflect on the situation and see things in a different light. She appreciated how fortunate she had been to have such a special friendship with Frida. She remembered that they had said, "they would be friends forever, no matter what happened."

Zelda's pain also lessened as she considered Frida's good fortune. She treasured her friend and knew that being with a family that loved her would bring Frida the joy and happiness she needed and unquestionably deserved.

Zelda also concluded that if Frida had been the one left behind, she would have had a more difficult time. It was obvious that Zelda was much better prepared to handle any future challenges that might arise in the jail-pound.

Chapter 8

Days later, a group of people came and looked through the jail-pound window. Zelda thrust herself in between two 12-pounders, hoping to emit her charm. She had ten seconds at the window before the big cats squeezed her out and the people were gone.

Gloomily, Zelda walked away from the window thinking that being stuck in this jail-pound forever might well be her fate. She yearned for some semblance of her old life at Pine Needle. Was this to be her life from now on, rotting away in a jail-pound with a bunch of stinky cats, with no Frida to love, yak and laugh with? And no Mark, Zeke and Zach who thoroughly adored her?

Out of the blue, the jail-pound manager appeared and picked her up. Zelda was carried to a table in an adjacent room. Sitting in nearby chairs were the people she had just seen through the window. The people said "Hi, Zelda Lou. How do you do?" Zelda proceeded to do what she always did when people seemed to be interested in what she had to offer. Using her charm, she meowed, walked up to each of them, purred (with rolled R's, her purring specialty) and looked them in the eye.

Zelda continued to present her most sociable and charming personality. Of the people looking on, one lady kept talking to her and petting her. She finally pulled Zelda onto her lap. It had been a long time since Zelda had been held and petted by a human. "That feels so good," she purred.

She was lifted up and placed in a cardboard box. The lid was closed, which upset her immensely. It wasn't that she minded the dark. She loved the nighttime; but she did not like being in the dark when the sun was out. Plus, she could barely move in this cramped space. She felt the box being carried, heard a car start up then realized she was moving. Could this be the start of her **third adventure**?

The ride lasted only 10 minutes. The box opened and "the lady" who had held her at the jail-pound was looking down at her. She stroked Zelda's head and ears and uttered sooth-ing words.

Zelda was about to leap into her arms when the lid closed again. She was being carried somewhere else. The box re-opened and Zelda peered out. She saw a different lady wearing a white coat with printed cat faces on it. Zelda whined. The white-coat lady spoke softly and then sang:

Hush little Zelda, do not cry.
Doc Lisa sings you a lullaby.

Doc Lisa looked into Zelda's mouth and ears and began poking her softly, at times in places Zelda did not appreciate. The lady was also there and observed everything that was done, apparently approving of it all. Before long, the lullabies stopped (Thank goodness!) and it was back in the box and off in the car again.

The next time the box opened, Zelda wasted no time and jumped out. Where was she? It was clearly a house, and not the trailer park of Pine Needle. She set out to explore, albeit cautiously.

Before she knew it, another cat was right in her face. The lady called him Henri. He was not exactly pleased to see Zelda, but he wasn't aggressive. There was no need for her expert survival skills to kick in. They just stared at each other.

Zelda was taken to another room and the lady closed the door behind her. It had been dark for some time, and it got very quiet, so the lady must have gone to bed. Zelda had the room to herself. There was a litter box and all the food and water she could want.

Finally, Zelda began to relax. "This isn't Pine Needle," she thought; "but at least I'm out of the jail-pound." She was very glad to be away from those other cats but also felt sorry that they remained imprisoned.

Zelda had no idea whether her life was going to change for the better; but so far, she felt safer and more secure than she had in weeks. As she settled into this calm and peaceful room, she began to groom herself, a luxury that had been impossible in the jail-pound with all the smelly cats bunched together. Eventually, Zelda fell sound asleep.

Zelda awakened the next morning to the lady gently calling her name and smiling at her. The lady's friends were there and all stared adoringly at Zelda. They held and petted her and gave Zelda their undivided attention. They showered her with cat toys and kitty treats. They all seemed to like everything she did. Zelda thought "They're as nice as Mark!"

As the day went on, the adulation continued. Zelda began to wonder, "Was this why Frida talked so longingly about her family? Is this my new family? Is this lady my Mommy? Will I get to sleep in the house every night and be fed twice a day? Will there be more treats and toys? If that's the case, Frida was right. This family thing is TOTALLY AWESOME." That night, Zelda had the best sleep of her life, totally content and happy. This lady was indeed her Mommy.

Chapter 9

Unbeknownst to Zelda, one of Mark's friends in Pine Needle had called him in California to tell him about the raid by Animal Control and Zelda's arrest. Mark immediately called the agency and asked that Zelda be held for him until he returned home; but they told him the rules stated cats could only be held for one day. It was impossible for Mark to return on such short notice, so his request was denied.

When Mark returned from California, he drove directly from the airport to the jail-pound and learned that Zelda had been adopted. He was heartbroken. She had meant more to him than he realized. With Zeke in Hollywood and Zelda adopted, he had lost two of his "3 Z's".

He hurried home to find Zach still at Pine Needle. Mark was ecstatic. He abandoned his earlier prohibition on cats being inside. "I'll just have to deal with cat hair." He brought Zach into the trailer and promised him that he would never leave. He hoped somehow that Zach understood. He showered Zach with love, which Zach gladly reciprocated.

Knowing how much Zach enjoyed mice hockey, Mark created field boundaries on the lawn and used strips of old badminton netting for the goal nets. With Zach's natural ability, as well as his large paws, he was often the star player for any team he was on.

Over time, Zach took on the role of coach and mentor to the younger, smaller cats who wanted to learn how to play. Zach emphasized training and taught drills and strategies that the cats used to improve their game.

Zach coached several divisional teams from Pine Needle. These teams excelled on the field and were invited to compete against trailer park teams from Southern Palms, Hard Cedar, Whispering Oaks and Maple Grove. Since Zach had the only real hockey field, games were usually played on his home turf. Zach's teams often won and everyone in Pine Needle enjoyed the matches.

The definition of success each year was to win the Big Mouse Trophy in the February Foolishness Tournament. Pine Needle's numerous victories garnered national attention in the big leagues of mice hockey and Zach was eventually named head coach of the Big Mouse Olympic team.

Chapter 10

Zelda liked her new family but felt conflicted. She had lived in the great outdoors her entire life and wasn't sure how she felt about living in a house. Zelda had the freedom to go in and out through a cat door but only in the daytime and then only when her Mommy was home. There was no nightlife for her to enjoy.

On top of that, Mommy would often come outside and call for Zelda to come home at the most inconvenient times. When that call came, Zelda might be stalking a bird, chasing a lizard, or playing with a snake. All that great fun stopped when Mommy called.

Zelda enjoyed this special attention but eventually began to resent it. "I've lived outside before and I can take care of myself." She yearned for more adventure, but also loved her life with Mommy and didn't want to break her rules.

After being taken from Pine Needle and then incarcerated in the jail-pound, Zelda wasn't as sure of herself as she had been previously. She fully realized that no matter how hard she prepared, things beyond her control could change her life in an instant. Zelda now seemed to worry about all sorts of things: "Will Mommy get tired of me? Will she take me back to the jail-pound? Will someone come and kidnap me away from here? Will Animal Control arrest me again?"

These trust issues and fears nagged at Zelda. She wasn't certain that life with Mommy and Henri would continue in such a positive way. Zelda had developed what some people call "separation anxiety," which created an insecurity she had never felt before.

One day while Mommy was away, Zelda was stuck in the house, totally bored. Searching for something to do, Zelda discovered that Mommy had not securely locked the cat door. Zelda jumped at the opportunity to pry it off and go out for some fun. "Hooray, I'm free for a while!" She looked back at Henri and invited him to join her. Henri responded dourly, "Are you kidding? It's against the rules!" Henri always followed rules to a tee. Zelda's **fourth adventure** was about to begin.

Zelda roamed for hours, loving every minute of it. She was not allowed to go into neighboring yards but did it anyway; exploring was in her blood. She was looking around so much that she failed to see a broken piece of glass right in front of her, and it sliced into her front paw. "Me-ow, Me-Ow OW OWW!" she wailed. Zelda limped home bleeding profusely just as Mommy returned home.

Zelda knew she would be in trouble for breaking the rules. However, she was not at all prepared for Mommy's reaction. In fact, Zelda had never seen her Mommy act like this.

Mommy scooped Zelda into her arms, ran to the house, put a rag on the bleeding paw, made a phone call and rushed Zelda to the car. "Oh no, she's taking me to the jail-pound." Zelda's paw really hurt and she was mortified that her actions had led to this. "Back to the pound with a paw I can't use. How will I fight if I need to?" Zelda was so freaked out she couldn't talk, which made the situation all the worse because Mommy wasn't talking either.

The car stopped. Mommy carried Zelda into a building and Zelda instantly recognized the lullaby-singing Doc Lisa in her white coat with cat faces. "Uh-oh. This can't be good," thought Zelda. Doc Lisa started singing:

Don't be afraid little Zelda Lou
Your Doc Lisa's here for you

Doc Lisa examined Zelda's paw. The next thing Zelda knew she was inside a small glass aquarium and fell asleep. She awoke in Mommy's arms to the sounds of Doc Lisa singing:

Old MacDonald had a farm, E-I-E-I-OH
And on his farm, he had two cats, E-I-E-I-OH
He named them Ralph and Susie Q
They talked to him saying Mew, Mew, Mew

Zelda thought, "Oh no. Now Doc Lisa's singing nursery rhymes." Mommy took Zelda home with a bandaged paw. It was still hurting, but not as badly; and there was no more blood.

Chapter 11

Zelda was determined to be more obedient and stay close to home. She was able to maintain that commitment for all of nine months, but then "the call of the wild" took over. Zelda gave in to temptation and **adventure number five** was right around the corner.

Mommy was gardening and Zelda was busy stalking some blue jays. The phone rang and Mommy went inside the house to answer it. Zelda turned away from the birds and spotted more than 50 squirrels in the yard across the street.

Everyone in the entire neighborhood knew that the squirrels on the other side of the street were easier to catch. Zelda understood she shouldn't, but the lure of that many squirrels was just too great. She raced across the street, aiming for the nearest squirrel, relishing every moment of her antici-pated conquest.

Within three minutes, every squirrel had hightailed it into the trees and was laughing at Zelda from 15 feet above her. Af-ter this failed escapade, Zelda started to run back across the street just as Mommy came out of the house. Zelda knew it! She was in trouble again.

Just then there was a loud roaring noise as a speeding car suddenly appeared. "NO, NO, NOOOO!" Mommy screamed. It was over in a split second. Mommy ran into the street, cry-ing hysterically. Where was her darling kitty? Had Zelda been carried away by that speeding car?

Zelda soon found herself in the middle of some bushes, with no idea how she got there. Her mind was muddled but she realized she was in her very own yard. Zelda slowly climbed out of the bushes and could hear Mommy calling. Mommy finally saw Zelda and looked at her in disbelief.

Mommy checked Zelda for blood. There was none. She in-spected every inch of Zelda's body. Nothing! Zelda didn't even muster an "Ouchie Meow." She just purred. Mommy was dumbfounded. Zelda walked with Mommy to the house, curled up in a chair and went to sleep.

Chapter 12

Although Zelda didn't fully understand what had happened or how she had survived the speeding car ordeal, she vowed to be more careful in the future. She stayed closer to home; but staying closer to home didn't prevent **adventure number six** because it materialized in her own yard.

Lizards were among the most fun creatures to play with in the yard and sometimes they even made a great snack. But chasing squirrels was much more fun and quite challenging.

On a balmy sunny day, just a few feet away, Zelda saw a squirrel sitting at the base of a tree. Zelda thought, "I got this one," and ran toward it. The squirrel darted up the tree, which split into two trunks six feet above the ground. The squirrel rested in the split, thinking he was safe; but Zelda made it to the split in one unbelievable jump. Startled, the squirrel quickly scampered even higher. From a branch 20 feet high, with Zelda in hot pursuit, the squirrel leapt onto the branch of a neighboring tree and was gone. "Wow!!" Zelda thought. "Wasn't that exciting? I really think chasing the squirrels is what makes it so much fun, even if I don't catch one."

Zelda carefully made her way toward the bottom of the tree and stopped when she saw a large male cat watching her from the ground. "Who's this guy?" She had never seen him before and he was huge, maybe even bigger than Growler. Then she remembered that Henri had told her about Big Tom, a new cat in the neighborhood; but Henri hadn't said if he was a friend or foe.

Zelda changed course and jumped onto the roof of a dilapidated shed next door. She was trying to figure out how to get down when she saw Big Tom right below her again. She quickly ran to the other side of the shed. Big Tom stayed on the ground and moved, yet again, to be directly below Zelda.

Zelda thought, "If he's a friend, he's sure not acting like one. "But boy is he big!!" Over the years, Zelda had gained several pounds and was stronger than before. Still, she hadn't been in a fight for a long time. With maturity, Zelda had also gained wisdom. She decided to wait a bit before forcing a direct confrontation with Big Tom. Zelda quietly moved to another side of the shed and looked down. From her new position, she could see Big Tom but he couldn't see her, and he remained on the side of the shed away from her.

Zelda heard Mommy calling but remained silent, not wanting to reveal her position. Mommy was searching everywhere, even across the street. Several times Mommy called Zelda's name while Zelda was right above her but Zelda wasn't about to respond with Big Tom so near. Zelda could tell by Mommy's voice that she was beginning to panic.

Mommy finally spotted Big Tom looking up toward the shed. When Mommy looked up, she saw her nervous Zelda. Mommy shooed Big Tom away, but Zelda realized there was no way she could get down by herself. Jumping up to the small branch from which she had leapt was too risky. Jumping to the ground wasn't an option either because the shed was surrounded by sticky palmetto bushes. She cried out for Mommy to rescue her.

Mommy ran to the garage and grabbed her only ladder, which was ten feet tall. She rested it against the 12-foot-high shed and started to climb even though it was clearly unsafe. Zelda came close to the edge then backed away, still scared. Mommy risked moving two rungs higher and reached toward Zelda, talking and singing to comfort her.

With whimpering meows, Zelda finally edged close enough for Mommy to grasp her. She placed Zelda in the fold of her arm and petted her head for a moment before starting down. Cautiously, Mommy stepped down the ladder while holding Zelda snugly. Zelda became impatient with the interminably slow pace and when they got to about six feet from the ground, she twisted out of Mommy's arm and jumped. Zelda was so relieved that she relieved herself right at the foot of the ladder.

Chapter 13

Zelda and Henri had become good friends even though he was not the least bit adventurous and followed the rules religiously. He just couldn't understand why Zelda wouldn't stay out of trouble as she kept going from one dramatic incident to another. Still, he had become protective of her. Every time she jumped through the cat door, Henri always meowed, "Be careful." Zelda would respond nonchalantly, "Sure, will do."

Once outside, Zelda would usually traipse to the edge of the backyard. On this day, she approached a large camellia bush and sensed another cat nearby. Zelda stopped and observed a white cat lying under the bush. He stood up when he saw Zelda, but then lay back down, a rather boring start to her **seventh adventure**.

Zelda kept her distance until she could ascertain who this intruder was and why he was there. "Hey, you. You're in my yard. Get out of here." He stood up again, walked three feet and then fell. Zelda noticed he was walking on three legs instead of four. He said "I'm hurt and trying to get home."

The white cat made several more attempts to walk but failed. "My name is Ghost and I live on your side street." Zelda introduced herself and asked, "If you live so close, why have I never seen you around here?" He replied, "Because there's a wall around our house."

Moving in closer, Zelda could see blood on his rear leg. "Oh, My! What happened?" Ghost replied, "Well, I'm pretty fast, but when I tried to cross the street, that car was even faster." Zelda realized that Ghost was definitely unable to go anywhere on his own. They talked a little longer until Mommy called.

As Zelda responded to Mommy's call, Ghost worriedly asked "You're gonna leave me here?" Zelda declared, "Of course not. I'll be right back." Zelda went to Mommy, who immediately picked her up, took her into the house and closed the cat door. Zelda tried to get Mommy's attention to tell her about Ghost, but Mommy was in a hurry. After Henri and Zelda were safely inside, Mommy got in the car and left.

Henri could tell Zelda was upset. "What's wrong?" he asked. Henri listened intently. Zelda said she couldn't just leave Ghost out there all night; she had given her word that she'd be back. Even so, there was nothing Zelda could do by herself.

Henri said, "OK. We'll figure out something together. But I can't believe you're tangled up in another crazy scheme and now you've got me involved in it too."

Henri checked the cat door. It was securely closed. Mommy had learned her lesson. Needing a plan, they began to brainstorm, tossing around so many ideas that even they knew they were too farfetched to work. Still, they kept thinking. One idea was to carry Ghost to his home. Or maybe they should go straight to his house and tell his Mommy. But what if they couldn't make her understand? Then what? They thoroughly discussed all of their ideas until Henri finally came up with something that seemed possible to execute.

As soon as Mommy returned and opened the cat door, Zelda and Henri bolted through it, running as fast as they could to Ghost. Zelda got there first. "Sorry I couldn't get back sooner. This is Henri. We have a plan to help you. Just sit tight." With a wry smile, Ghost (noting the obvious) jokingly said "Ok. If you insist, I'll stay here with you." They all laughed.

It was getting dark. Henri and Zelda knew Mommy would soon be calling them home. Before long, they heard her voice. Henri came out from under the camellia bush and sat down where he could be seen. Zelda waited with Ghost.

After a few minutes, Mommy set out to find the pair. She checked the front yard first calling out "Henri. Zelda Lou." Then she entered the backyard and saw Henri. "There you are. Come on in now." He didn't move. After a moment, he ran back under the bush. This irritated Mommy because she was used to her cats following her directions, especially Henri. Mommy looked under the bush and saw Ghost sandwiched between Henri and Zelda. Curious, she reached for Ghost first and immediately saw the blood.

She was alarmed but, as always, knew exactly what to do. She went to the house, retrieved a cat carrier and put a bowl of food inside. Hurrying back, she placed the open carrier door right next to Ghost's face. He hesitated. "Well, what are you waiting for?" coaxed Zelda. He limped into the carrier and Mommy closed the door. Ghost gulped down the food and they all went into the house. Zelda congratulated Henri. "Good plan! You knew Mommy would find him if we didn't come when she called for us."

Mommy remembered seeing a "Cat Missing" flyer on a telephone pole and went to read it. Sure enough, a beautiful picture of Ghost was at the bottom. Mommy telephoned the owner, a Mrs. Zimmerman, and said "I think we've found your Ghost, but he's badly hurt."

Mrs. Zimmerman rushed to Mommy's house. Upon seeing Ghost and his injury, she immediately started to cry. She thanked Mommy profusely as she gently lifted her cat and cradled him in her arms. Mommy gave all the credit to Zelda and Henri. Mrs. Zimmerman bent down and petted both of them, saying "Thank you so much." Henri proudly puffed up his chest and Zelda purred with her rolled R's.

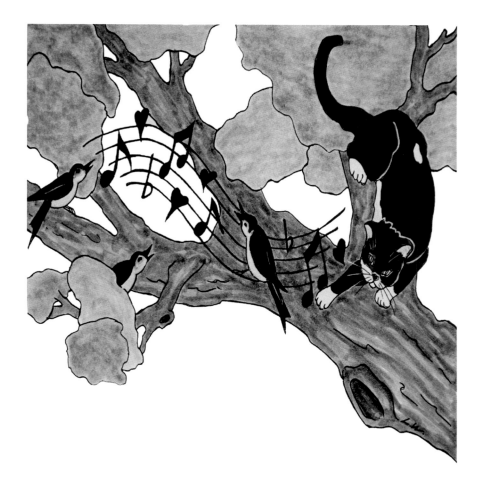

Chapter 14

Zelda was happy and content with her life. She adored Mommy and Henri and had a large yard to play in. All the squirrels, garden snakes, birds, and other wildlife made life interesting and exciting. Zelda especially liked the challenge of catching moles. Plus, Mommy gave her extra cat treats after each capture. When the whole family was outside together, Mommy would sing:

My cats are the very best cats one can have
Playing in the yard, they make my life less hard

Zelda loved Mommy's singing. In fact, she loved everything about her life because all was going very well. That's why Zelda's **eighth adventure** was almost tragic. Zelda was climbing trees and having a blast trying to see how close she could get to the five birds singing sweetly in the tallest tree in the yard. She was just about to step onto the branch with the birds when she heard a strange noise. Suddenly she hit the ground, stunned and confused.

Zelda cried out for Mommy, who heard her. Mommy found Zelda near the oak trees, not moving. Zelda's head had never hurt this badly. Mommy lifted her up and took her inside to her bed. She petted Zelda and poked around her body like before, but this time Zelda was in too much pain to utter any "Ouchie Meows."

Within an hour, Zelda found herself in front of that lullaby singing Doc Lisa again:

Looks like Zelda took a fall
I will help 'cause you're a doll

Mommy left the room and Zelda panicked. This must mean she was being left with lullaby singing Doc Lisa for good. Her anxiety about being abandoned took over any rational thinking on her part. She was certain Mommy had decided she didn't want or need a cat so clumsy it could fall out of a tree.

Should Zelda try to charm Doc Lisa? At least being with her would be better than the jail-pound. Then Doc Lisa started singing again. Now, Zelda prayed hard for Mommy to come back, forgive her for falling out of a tree and take her home. The door opened and it was Mommy! As Doc Lisa spoke, Mommy looked concerned. Zelda was seven years old now, and she understood a lot of people words, but she had never heard these words before: X-ray, BB gun, and concussion. Tears began falling from Mommy's eyes and running down her cheeks. Doc Lisa comforted Mommy with another one of her lullabies:

Zelda's BB won't cause any harm
Just take her home where it's safe and warm

Mommy held Zelda in her lap as they drove home, something she had never done before. She took Zelda to her bed, lying close beside her with Zelda's paw in her hand. Henri jumped up to be with them. He licked Zelda's forehead between her ears showing how much he cared for her.

Zelda felt so loved and comforted, she now knew without a doubt, Mommy and Henri really loved her and would never abandon her. She remembered Frida talking about her close-knit family and how "perfect" it was. Finally, Zelda knew exactly what she meant.

Chapter 15

It took time for Zelda to recuperate from the concussion. But shortly thereafter, the **ninth adventure** unfolded. Mommy, Zelda and Henri were outside on an unusually cold day. Un-expectedly, a large and mean-looking dog ran into their yard barking loudly. All of them were terrified.

Mommy shouted for Zelda and Henri as she darted into the house. She saw Henri jump through the cat door. Mommy didn't see Zelda outside and figured she had beaten them to the house. She looked everywhere inside, but Zelda wasn't there.

Mommy returned to the backyard and called for Zelda. The dog was gone, but Zelda was nowhere to be seen. She seemed to have vanished in an instant. Mommy took Henri with her to scour the neighborhood. Zelda was nowhere to be found.

Mommy made flyers with a picture of Zelda. Mrs. Zimmerman helped her post them all over the neighborhood. Mommy expected to get a call quickly, but that didn't happen. Now, it was well after dark. Mommy and Henri were worried sick. They stayed up most of the night, hoping for Zelda's return.

The next day, Zelda remained missing and Mommy was completely distraught. Another search of the neighborhood turned up nothing. Mommy and Henri tried to console each other, but they were miserable without Zelda. Not knowing what had happened to her made it even worse.

On the third day, Henri was moping about outside when suddenly, Zelda came running toward him. She seemed uninjured and perfectly fine. Henri screeched at her: "Where've you been? Was this another one of your escapades? Do you know what you've put us through? I can't believe you did this!"

Zelda didn't get upset. She was too excited to see Henri and finally be home again. Zelda told Henri that when she saw the dog, she was close to the neighbor's garage and ran there to hide. "The next thing I knew, they closed the garage door, and I was stuck inside."

Zelda said, "I searched everywhere for a way out, but it was impossible. The windows were nailed shut and the garage door had a lock on it. But the garage door opened just now and I ran as fast as I could to get here."

Henri apologized for being so accusatory. "I'm glad you're home safe and sound. Mommy has been miserable. She

thought the dog must have gotten you. Either that or you had died outside in the freezing cold."

"Come on," Henri said. They ran to the house and jumped through the cat door. Mommy, seated at the kitchen table, was weeping with her head in her hands. Zelda and Henri jumped up onto the table. Mommy leapt to her feet and scooped them both up. She was still crying, but it was a different cry, a smiling and laughing cry. "Zelda schweeta, we thought you were never coming home." Henri meowed and Zelda purred with her rolled R's. Mommy didn't want to ever let them go, but knew Zelda must be starving. Indeed, she was.

Zelda was treated to the best meal ever. Usually a picky eater, she devoured everything Mommy put in front of her. Henri shared in the feast. They stayed up late into the night, playing and loving on each other. Zelda fell asleep in Mommy's bed, cuddled between her and Henri. Zelda's odyssey had led her to a life she could never have imagined and a future that would be filled with countless happy days with her very own "perfect family."

CAT CROSSING →

THE END

ACKOWLEDGEMENTS

I am most grateful for the assistance of the following people, without whom *Zelda's Odyssey* would not have been possible:

Barbara Barber
Cherie Coddington
Julie Hancock
Stan Kyker
Steve Maddox
Cappy Hall Rearick
Randolph Russell
Linda Wunder

And thanks to Dr. Lisa J. Ryan, a St. Simons Island veterinarian, for allowing me to use her "singing persona" as Zelda's "Doc Lisa."